Himalayan Cookbook

Recipes of the Nutrition, Cuisine, and Culture

By

Makar Jang Rai

Edited by

Liam UiCearbhaill

This book is dedicated to Donald Brant, who encouraged me to write this book. He is a very good friend.

Himalayan Cookbook

Copyright 2018

Makar Jang Rai

Cover painting and some images courtesy of Bimal Rai and Kami Sherpa

To contact the author:

Makarrai954822@gmail.com

ISBN-13: 978-1724786494

ISBN-10: 1724786490

Camp Four on Mount Everest. Picture by Kami Sherpa.

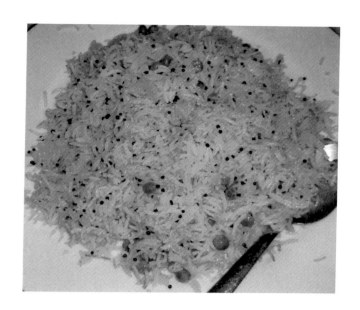

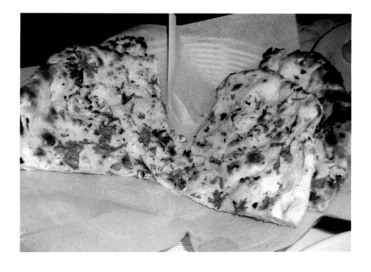

Table of Contents

FOOD

In Nepal most of the cooking is done by the mother. Occasionally the father prepares food for the family, when the mother visits her Maiti Ghar (Maiti = Brother, Ghar = House, idiomatically her birth home) during festival times. Nepalese women do not traditionally cook during menstruation. Mothers teach all of their kids how to cook the food and how to survive in the Himalayas, especially in the Winter. Sometimes during yak herding in the mountains snow can fall four feet in one hour, so "giving up never works". Our parents teach us to follow the direction and keep moving yourself to join the family and hot food. Animal herding is challenging in the jungle where there are foxes, wild dogs, bear, and tigers. Always carry a sharp khukuri (Nepalese knife) to protect yourself and the herd. Sometimes you meet other herders and will play games and sports. Sometimes you meet with girl herders and they have red cheeks and natural beauty which makes a beautiful day go quickly. Nepalese people respect mother as a goddess and father as a god.

A Himalayan daughter is respected as a Debi which means "bright young goddess in the house". She brightens the house, and also learns from her mother, and helps her.

In the Himalayas, sons defends the family and the country. In our festival, Dashain, our father and grand-father tell us, "be strong defend the family and the country, and be honest". This is the blessing we receive every year from childhood to young age, listening to those words over the years positively affects our lives. In the Himalayas we live as an extended family so someone is always available to cook for the family.

My grandfather was a shaman. He would treat people's problems using his shamanic knowledge. He was respected because he could heal people's spirits. He sometimes had to struggle with witches and devils in order to heal the victims. He was treated as a god and given the best food and respect for the healings he performed.

He acquired recipes for the foods he liked the most and taught the recipes to his family.

He also connected to the Divine to ask how to conduct his healings. The Divine would guide him. He would communicate by asking the Divine for detailed knowledge about how to treat the person who needed to be healed.

In Nepal the family gets the general food cooked by the mother. The father gets special food, his favorite dishes. I was influenced by my father's recipes. He would cook the rooster with spices, like turmeric, cumin, coriander, ajwan, bay leaf, garlic, ginger, plus tomato and onion.

He would give us sautéed rooster, cooked for two hours in a slow wood fire, using three stones over an open fire, cooked slowly in a cooking pot called a karai. He would give this to his family. The food was so delicious I cannot forget it. When it was served, it was aromatic and savory. He cooked the food with love. To eat such a meal connected the family together. This was a spiritual experience for the family and was healthy for the body and mind. His cooking was of the highest level.

He prepared gravy with cooking spices combined with meat juices to give the food a rich taste, like the best orchestra. You can feel the fresh spices around your tongue and your palate and all your senses.

We ate meat only once a week or sometimes once in fifteen days. Most of the food consisted of vegetables and grain, like rice or wheat.

I learned my cooking skills from my parents. When I was in the Gurkhas I learned more about seafood, vegetables, and barbecue cooking. I cooked for my friend in the messing (as in "mess hall"). Everything was cooked fresh and my friend was called to join us. After the messing there was music, singing and dancing. A party! This is a part of our culture that helps us to feed our bodies and heal our minds.

We prepared the livestock because the cooking required everything to be fresh. In Nepal we cooked the meat with fresh spices. The second day the spices would soak into the food and bring out the flavor even more so we would cook enough to last for up to three days.

The livestock we would cook and eat was always the livestock from the farm. The most active ram or rooster was always chosen. If you eat the most active animal you acquire that animal's energy for your spirit. In the Himalayas the air is clean, cold and fresh. Bacteria do not grow in cold weather. The cold air makes the animals very active and keeps fruits and vegetables very fresh. There are many herbs which can be used for medicine, longevity and increased intelligence. Drinking yak blood can cure many sicknesses, possibly including cancer.

Fruits and vegetables in Nepal take longer to grow and harvest, from six to eight months. This makes for more nutritious crops for the harvest. The people of Nepal are very healthy, seldom sick, do not suffer from obesity and do not get cancer. They do not suffer from Alzheimer's syndrome when they get older.

All crops are grown organically from compost to give the food extra nutrition. We work our farms manually in the mountains and people are very happy and healthy because of this. They express their respect toward others by saying "Namaste", which means: "I salute the God within You." If anyone comes to your house, they receive respect equal to that of a God. The good food and mountain scenery, their love of the family and respect for order, make the people of Nepal very happy.

TRADITIONS AND NUTRITION

A million years ago our ancestors had small heads and sometimes lived short lives. Thousands of years passed. Instead of eating only the food that was available, people began to cultivate food of many different varieties, giving them a broader diet. In Japan people eat fish and seaweed for variety. In mainland Asia, from China to India, people use grains, herbs and vegetables to give their diet more nutrition. In Europe people raised and ate cattle, which also gave them butter, milk and cheese. In Iceland and the Arctic, people ate fish. The Hindu people don't eat cows. They worship their cows instead.

After the two great wars fought by the Europeans, sicknesses like polio appeared and cost many people their lives. Doctors did not know how to treat these diseases. Scientists discovered medicines that were used to cure these diseases and doctors studied diet. They discovered vitamins. They learned how food gives us nutrition and how our diet can keep us healthy.

Free-ranging cattle and free flocks of chickens give us meat that is healthy and contains very little fat. Animals kept in pens and cages are not as healthy for us to eat. They have too much fat and their muscles aren't strong.

If you know what you are eating now, it is because scientists have discovered the nutrients in the various types of food. Knowing that, you can improve your life, your sight, your mind, and the health of your body. Scientific research from all over the world will be included in this book. People have improved their health by following the advice I have given them. Many people encouraged me to write this book so I can share the research I have done. This book contains my own research about the food we eat, the right amount to eat, the calories and vitamins the food contains, and when we should eat certain foods. This information can be used to improve health and strength. You will learn how to cook, how much to eat, how the food works for you, what quantities of nutrition you need, how many calories you need, and how much energy you burn living your daily life.

Nepal is a sovereign country for all time. Nepal is situated between India and China. Siddhartha Gautam Buddha was born in Nepal more than 2,500 years ago. The beautiful Himalayas, tallest mountains in the world, are in Nepal, including Mount Everest. Sherpas and Gurkhas are from Nepal. Nepal is a multicultural and multi-tribal system. 130 different languages are spoken in Nepal. Nepalese soldiers fought alongside the British in World War One and World War Two. The Nepalese government sent 10,000 soldiers to the British army, plus 100,000 to India and 5,000 to Brunei, which is located next to Malaysia. Today almost 10,000 Nepalese police help protect Singapore. They are the people called the Gurkhas. The Gurkhas police force provided security during a summit between the U.S. President Donald Trump and North Korean Leader Kim Jong Un.

2,800 years ago the Kirati tribe established a kingdom in Nepal. The first king was Yulambar. This was during the Dvapara Yug, (according to Sanskrit literature, a time when God was still active and practiced compassion and truthfulness). Thirty-two Kirati kings have ruled the country. They ruled until the 3rd Century A.D.

The Lichhivi people established a friendship with the king. By combining treachery and persuasion with alcohol, they took over the kingdom. The Lichhivi Dynasty ruled for three centuries. The king, whose name was Ansubharma, married his daughter to the king of Tibet to avoid a trade war. Nepal traded salt and medicine with Tibet.

The Thakuri Dynasty overthrew the Lichhivi Dynasty. The Thakuri Dynasty was overthrown by the Malla Dynasty. The Malla king tried to impose Hinduism and the caste system. The people rejected this and the country split into 24 small states. This was in the 15th Century. The Malla Dynasty ended in the 17th Century.

The father of Prithibi Narayan Shaha wanted to reunite the country because of trade problems with India, caused by the British occupation. When his father died, Prithibi started a war to unify Nepal. He took Kathmandu in 1768. There were many more states to subdue. He negotiated with the Kiratis to unite against the British. The Shaha Dynasty worked very hard to reunite the country because of the mistakes of the Malla Dynasty.

Kathmandu had many big trees. Kathmandu means "Holy City of Trees." In the Tibetan language "ne" means "wool" and "pal" means house, so "Nepal" means "house of wool." However, in the Newari Bhasa language, "Nepa" means "country in the middle zone," or "Nepal."

Nepal went to war against Tibet in the 1780s. It was a trade war. Nepal supplied coins to Tibet, which were the cause of the war. Tibet requested support from China for support in the conflict. Nepal lost. China tried to conquer Nepal and failed. This resulted in a treaty.

Nepal took the northern part of India, up to the Ganga River. The British who occupied India wanted to take back the area north of the river. The British fought the Nepalese and reclaimed the region, including the southern part of Nepal. The British tried to conquer Nepal but failed. They were defeated by Gurkhas, led by the general Bhakti Thapa. The British wrote a treaty instead. This was negotiated from 1814 to 1816, the Anglo-Nepal War.

In 1848 Janga Bahadar Rana plotted the Kot Parba Massacre. He killed all of the princes and imprisoned the king. He appointed himself to be prime minister and usurped the power. He denied human rights and education. He sent Nepalese boys to the British government, to serve in India.

The British had tried to recruit Nepalese boys into their military. They were impressed by Nepalese fighting skills. They tried to negotiate with the Nepalese government so they could use Nepalese boys to fight for the British Empire.

After World War Two the British had to leave India in 1947. The underground Nepalese congress in India planned a revolution to topple the Jahania Rana rule. In 1950 King Tribhuwan Birabikram Shaha Dev fled to India. An armed revolt of the Nepalese people killed Rana and his family. Some fled the country.

In 1951 the king became absolute ruler of the country. In 1955 the king died and his first son, Mahendra Birabikram Shaha Dev replaced him on the throne. The people did not like the king's parliamentary politics. They revolted. An election was held in 1959 and the leader of the Nepalese congress, B. P. Koirala became the first democratically elected prime minister. He ruled for one year. Then the king took over political power and imprisoned the politicians. The king accused them of corruption and said the political parties were not working together. The king established the Panchayat Parliament in 1960. He died in 1979. His son Birendra succeeded to the throne.

In 1990 the people rebelled against the king and fifty people died. An election was held and another democratic constitution was written under the king. The Maoist Communist Party did not like the constitutions and went to war with the king and opposing political parties. The war began in 1996 and ended in 2006. 15,000 people were killed. King Birendra and his family were attacked and killed in their palace in the Darbar Massacre in 2001. Because of that event many people fled the country. King Gyanendra Birabikram Shaha Dev became king. He was a younger brother of the late king. He placed political leaders under house arrest and usurped the power. In April, 2006, the people rebelled and went on strike for 19 days. 16 people were killed before the king surrendered. The 240-year Shaha Dynasty came to an end. A new constitution was drawn up after an election was held. This process began in 2008 and finally completed in 2017. It established a federal secular parliamentary republic divided into seven provinces. Nepal did not have local, state and federal governments before this election.

The government of India did not like the Nepalese constitution and imposed sanctions against Nepal. An earthquake struck in 2015. Those two years were very painful for the Nepalese people.

The Nepalese people are pure in spirit because they are a sovereign country for all time. The four main political parties that make up the Nepalese Congress are the AML or United Mao and Lenin Principles, Maoist Communist Party, Sangia Samajbadi Forum and the RJP, or Rastiya Janta Party. There are many other small parties. At this point the structure of Nepalese politics is perfect according to the demands of the people. If the politicians of Nepal manage good governance and take care of the people, the country will be wealthy, beautiful and peaceful. Many people believe that Nepal is like the Switzerland of Asia.

Nepal has flat plains to the south, which are very fertile. Many rivers flow through there. Half of Nepal is mountainous, with the Himalayas in the north. 29,500,000 people live in Nepal. The national language is Nepali. The people are multicultural, multilingual, and share many customs because they are peaceful and compatible. The cuisine is different from region to region. Everyone gets along with everyone else. They are the happiest of people. They are very spiritual and believe that all people contain a personal God within them.

PERSONAL HISTORY

I was born in Hong Kong in 1966. My mother did not want to let the nurse separate me from her because many times boy babies are exchanged for girls. China had a one-child policy then. I was the second child and first son of my parents. In our family culture sons are important to continue the family dynasty.

My parents took me to a mountain village at two years of age. This was in the region of Mount Everest. Solma was the name of the village. The weather there was cold. The warmest it ever got was about 70 degrees Fahrenheit in the summer. The air was fresh and the mountains were forested.

My parents taught me how to work on a farm with animals. I learned everything I could about animals, from their character to our connections with them. All animals have different characters and habits. You must know how to play with them. All the animals will recognize you. I had a lot of love and connection with the animals. We had a cow, some sheep, goats, pigs, chickens and a buffalo, plus cats and dogs.

Our home was beautiful. I grew up with four brothers and a sister, my mother and father, grandmother and my paku auntie, my father's second sister. Everybody worked on the farm manually. We grew corn, potatoes, wheat, buckwheat, millet, mustard, cauliflowers, cabbages, onions, taro, nettles, mustard greens and radishes.

People of the Himalayas work hard and eat a lot, so they sleep well. My mother told me to work as a laborer and eat like a king. I became a hard worker and a good eater. Hard work pays the cost of good food. My religion is respect for our parents, our ancestors, which we call pitri, and respect for the Earth.

My first school's name was Nimna Madyamic Bidhyalaya Khidima. It was a secondary high school. I started going to school when I was seven years old.

We would get up at six o'clock in the morning to hike four to eight miles uphill to gather food for the animals. We gathered the leaves of the khasur trees, as well as grass. After coming down as far as eight miles we ate a quick lunch before going to school for two hours. School started at ten o'clock in the morning. From twelve to one o'clock we had a recess and we finished the school day at four o'clock in the afternoon. We came back in time to help our parents feed the animals. We ate dinner at eight in the evening. Then we did homework for two hours by the light of a kerosene lantern. There was no electricity and no television.

The Nepalese education passing mark is 32 points out of 100. We would never feel tired or lazy after working so hard. The food we ate made us strong.

At school I learned how to work with friends in society. I went to Dharan to attend high school. The name of the school was Horesh Cadoori High School, but now it has been changed to Depot Higher Secondary School, Dharan Ghopa Camp.

I was enlisted in the British Gurkha in 1985, this is a part of the British Army made up of Nepalese young men. To join the Gurkha requires intense competition. Almost 5 million boys from the hills compete to join. They are tested mentally and physically. I took up wrestling, which is called lappa. I threw my opponent down and broke his arm. Wrestling is popular in Nepal. Military officers and dignitaries were watching that match. I served for 16 years and then retired. I lived in Nepal for two years and came to America in 2002.

Food in America is very bland to me. I didn't like the taste of American food. I really tried to remember my parent's cooking. Even meat, vegetables and eggs are not tasty. Forget about the spices. We cook at home in America with spices that are not fresh. It is less than one-third the taste of food in the Himalayas. I used to cook for my friends, who encouraged me to open a restaurant.

I opened a business in 2004 called Himalayan Café, where I cooked with fresh spices, vegetables and meats. I also used the local products like chickens, lamb, bison, fruits and vegetables. I also introduced Nepalese culture to the local people, because I enjoy sharing my food and culture, and nourishing the community. I teach my culinary art at the Ukiah School District Nutrition Program and at the Ukiah Farmer's Market. I enjoy being in the community because of my food and culture. I want to teach my skill to Nepalese earthquake victims, especially the orphans. I recommend studying the Food Manager book for safe food handling. This can be found on Google and the Environmental and Health Department of most US counties.

TESTIMONIALS

"In 2010 I was privileged to be introduced to the Himalayan Café in Ukiah, California, and its owners. I had no previous experience with Nepalese culture or cuisine. In the following seven years, my life, as well as my tongue, have been blessed by the culture as well as the cuisine. When I think of all my culinary experiences, none can come close to the impact Nepalese cuisine has had on my life in the kitchen and my life outside the kitchen as well.

"My favorite dish has become lamb vindaloo. I like this dish extra spicy and when I eat this dish I truly experience the spices used to create this unique flavor palate. Paprika, cumin, garam marsala are all now much more emotional to me than other spices.

"In seven years I have shared my experience with countless friends, each time generating the same response: 'This is the real Ukiah'."

--Stephen MacLean

"I am so happy to have a loyal customer become a good friend. Steve and his girlfriend like very spicy food which builds up the same kind of chemistry in both of them. They are always happy and enjoy life. He would like to visit Nepal with me in the future."

--Rai

"I love Indian/Nepalese food. The tastes are enlivening and I enjoy the distinct flavors and textures. Add to that the health benefits of the seasonings, what more could I ask for? Rai's restaurant and cuisine has been a gift to our small town.

"Today I enjoyed the Himalayan mix of chicken and lamb with vegetables and rice in a delightful sauce. Delicious!"

--Marcella Ries

"Marcella used to come when I had a buffet but she stopped coming after I closed the buffet. She started coming back when her body began to crave the spices. The magnet of the spices dragged her back to the restaurant. "

--Rai

"The Himalayan Café is a wonderful compliment to dining in Ukiah. We first heard about the Himalayan on the local public radio station and it piqued our interest. Wandering in there for the first time we felt transported to a rustic, exotic place, surrounded by reminders of the giant 'roof of the earth.' The food is wonderful—boneless lamb in a tomato cream sauce or chicken mango, the garlic naan flat-breads, the curry sauces, the deft use of ginger and saffron, and Nepalese spices. We have many wonderful memories of the Himalayan Café, as it became the place to celebrate anniversaries and other milestones in our lives."

--Steve Scalmanini and Annie Esposito

"Steve used to be mayor of the town of Ukiah, where he is now a councilman. He is an activist on the Climate Change issue. This is good for Kirati families because they worship the planet. He and Annie became good friends. He and his wife are happy and charming people."

--Rai

"A wonderful work of ideas and recipes from a far, exotic region.

"Rai was instrumental in introducing Nepalese cuisine to our area. We frequented his restaurant when it opened in 2004. The exotic spices and aroma stimulated our senses. The fire on our tongues required quenching with cold Indian beer. The whole experience was unforgettable. With his guidance in this book, we can at least try to recreate that experience.

"In 2004, a Tsunami devastated part of southern India. We invited dancers from India to perform and raise funds to provide relief for the victims. Rai generously provided food and donated dinners in this effort. His generosity helped build an orphanage for victims in that region.

Let's celebrate this remarkable work."

Theron Chan M.D.

Dr Chan went to India for the tsunami relief effort with the Ukiah Rotary Club and Indian Rotary Members. He has a lot of compassion for the orphans.

Rai

Connect the community

As we do business in a community it is vital to connect with the local people. Sometimes a specific day of work is more exhausting then a whole week of work. It is good to express your stress to your family. A proactive spouse may take you to a restaurant and order your favorite food with extra turmeric and extra hot and spicy to sweat out the negative energy of the day. As a community we can feel, heal, and nurture the community. We all need help and love, without it all of us are very weak. I have many good memories in Ukiah about gratitude, love, and healing in the community.

I built a stage in the restaurant, and offer local people the opportunity to perform their music and dance. So far Belly Dancing has become very popular. I did a Nepalese culture talk, performed music and dance and served special cultural food and drinks, and the restaurant became a cultural destination in the town. More than oneself, sharing with others can touch peoples' hearts. Dancing once a month is good for your soul.

What is a spice?

Spices are mostly seeds, roots, stems, buds, and flowers which come from plants. They are above the level of normal food. Spices have strong taste, texture, aroma, healing power, vitamins, color and character. If you taste the spices black cardamom and timbur, they are very strong. They help to make the food beautiful in color and flavor. Spices are the game-changer for the flavor of the food. It is a precious gift from nature, discovered thousands of years ago. Nepalese people cannot live without spices. The Nepalese food motto is "tarkari mitho masalale hunchha." That means curry will be tasty just through the spices. People of the Himalayas are happy and enjoy the spice of life.

Turmeric: It has antibacterial, anti-inflammatory, antioxidant properties and is anti-aging. In Asian ritual we use turmeric for cleansing and to purify the spirit. In Nepal turmeric is used to heal open wounds and internal bleeding. It is also used to alleviate colds and arthritis. It is also useful for marijuana overdose.

Paprika: is anti-cholesterol. It also imparts natural color to the food. When paprika is cooked with turmeric, the mixture turns brown. This doubles the healing power of both.

Ajwan: has a good aroma and contains good healing power. It can help a young mother have enough milk to nurse her babies. It is good for pain relief and alleviates gastric problems. It can be added to curry, soup, and cooked with wine to warm your body in the winter.

Garam masala: the name means "heat through the power of the spice." Garam masala heats and stimulates the body. It opens blocked blood vessels. Garam masala consists of clove, cinnamon, black cardamom, bay leaves, black pepper, coriander and cumin.

Cumin: this spice imparts the best aroma. It is also anti-inflammatory. Cumin can be cooked with rice, curry and can be ground and used as a seasoning. This is the main spice featured in the movie, *Hundred Yard Journey*.

Coriander: gives out a fragrant aroma, plus it helps with anxiety and digestion. It should always be mixed with cumin to balance the flavor.

Sesame seeds: good for hair growth and skin protection. They can be used for pickling.

Fenugreek: one of the best aromatic spices. When heated in oil, cooked until dark brown, releasing oil and fragrance, fenugreek is very unique. It is high in nutrition and good for kidney stones and gallstones. It is anti-diabetic. It can be cooked into curry, rice and bread.

Nutmeg: good for digestion, helps to cook the bones in meat faster. It increases sexual activity. Taking too much is harmful. Use just a small amount for best results.

Asafoetida: protects the body from influenza, helps digestion, shortens cooking time.

Onion: this is a great spice with anticancer properties, relieves itching, headaches and is antibacterial.

Garlic: is another great spice with antibacterial properties. It is high in Omega 3.

Ginger: is a third great spice that attacks harmful bacteria. It alleviates nausea and vomiting during pregnancy. It elevates people.

Bay leaf: high in antioxidants. Good when added to curry, rice and tea.

Curry leaves: high in antioxidants and beta carotene. It has the best aroma.

Saffron: can treat depression, Alzheimer's disease and uplift your feelings. It is the most expensive spice. It is grown in Iran, Kashmir and Spain. It has a beautiful aroma and color.

Chili: there are many kinds of chili throughout the world. Some are hot and some are mild. Ghost pepper, habanero and Thai chili are very strong. This can be measured on a scale called the British Unit. Ghost peppers are almost one million units. Bell peppers are zero units. Chili is made hot because of capsaicin. Chili is good for pain relief, arthritis, neck pain and prevention of blood clots. It also kills bad bacteria in the intestine and it prevents frostbite if you put it in your socks. The Sherpa people eat the hottest chili in the world.

Sichuan pepper: there are many varieties of Sichuan peppers. In Nepal we call them timbur. They are very strong to your tongue, lemony and chillingly sparkling hot. They are high magnesium and iron. We use these spices to heat our bodies in the winter.

Nepal, India, Bangladesh and Pakistan all use these spices in their cuisine. Spices kill all the bad bacteria and increase the flavor of the food. When ordering food at a restaurant, always ask for extra turmeric and chili. Eating these spices every day cleans your body and makes you healthy.

BHUTEKO MAKAI BHATMASS   [Soybeans & Corn Sauté]

Breakfast

Sauteed corn and soybeans

Fried kernels of corn and whole soybeans are good for breakfast to serve four people.

12 oz. dried kernels organic corn

6 oz. dried organic soybeans

½ teaspoon ghee (purified yak butter)

Pinch of salt

30 oz. buttermilk or jar (Nepalese saki)

Clay pot and bamboo sticks

Cook corn in a heated clay pot with a small neck. This will trap the heat with the corn. Heat the clay pot for one minute and then put the corn in it. Stir with bamboo sticks for three minutes. Add the soybeans and continue stirring for five more minutes. Add a pinch of salt and ghee. When the grains have turned slightly reddish-brown in color, take it out of the pot and spread on a flat plate to cool for five minutes. Serve it with buttermilk for the children or jar for the adults.

Health benefits: minerals from corn include: 15% iron and 30% magnesium. Soybeans are high in fiber, vitamin K, omega three compounds, and minerals. Whole soybeans and corn strengthens teeth.

THEPLE BHAT   [Corn Rice]

Lunch

Theple bhat is a corn mush for the afternoon meal.

Corn mush is very popular in the Himalayas. To prepare it you must first grind the corn in a stone grinder, which is called a jhato. Corn is ground into three categories; powdery, medium and large pieces. Large pieces plus powdered corn, cooked together, is called theple. Medium-sized corn granules are called chekhla and cooked separately. Corn pieces and corn powder can be purchased in whole food stores here in the U.S.

Recipe for Theple Bhat to serve four people:

Ingredients:

20 oz. of large pieces of corn immersed in water for 20 minutes

10 oz. of corn flour

2 liters of water

One large pot and ladle

Heat a large pot, add water and bring to a boil. Add the large pieces of corn. Cook for 20 minutes and then add the corn flour. Stir the mixture for five minutes with a strong wooden ladle. Put the lid on the pot and cook for another five minutes over a very slow fire. The corn will turn to a whitish-brown color when it is ready to be served. It goes well with a nettle curry and tin pane raksi, a home-made Himalayan vintage.

Health benefits include: corn, high in minerals and vitamins, vitamin B-6, which gives energy and boosts protein metabolism. It helps calm nerves, maintains the nervous system and supports the adrenal functions.

KODOKO DHERO   [Millet Mush]

Lunch or Dinner

Millet can be ground with a stone-grinding mill to make flour. We can make four dishes out of the flour. They are bread, mush, soup and mess. This recipe can be also used for corn mess, buckwheat mess and wheat mess.

This is the recipe for kodoko dhero, enough to serve three people:

16 oz. millet flour

1 liter of water

3 teaspoons of ghee (purified buffalo butter)

Medium iron pot with cooking ladle

Heat the pot. Fill it with water and bring to a boil. Add the flour while stirring with a strong, wooden ladle. Continue stirring for five minutes, hard and vigorously, to prevent the flour from sticking to the inside of the pot. Put the lid on the pan and cook for five more minutes over a slow fire. When you smell the aroma, it is ready to be served. It is made to go with fish curry. Make a small hole in the top of each portion to pour the ghee into. Serve with red wine. That combination purifies the liver.

Benefits: high in minerals and vitamins. Good for growing children. Contains iron, high fiber, and is gluten free.

DHANKO BHAT [Basmati Rice]

Rice

There are many kinds of rice. Basmati rice has the highest level of taste within the rice family. Rice from the Himalayas has more flavor and aroma. If you cook basmati rice you can smell the fragrance at a distance. Basmati means "aromatic". If you visit basmati rice fields in the foothills of the mountains, your nostrils will be filled with the basmati rice aroma.

Dhanko Bhat is a meal that can be prepared for either lunch or dinner. This recipe can be used to cook different kinds of rice. This recipe will yield servings for three people.

16 oz. organic basmati rice immersed in one liter of water for 30 minutes.

2 tablespoons of ghee or olive oil

½ teaspoon of salt

¼ teaspoon of cumin seeds

A pinch of saffron or turmeric

1 liter of water

Medium-sized cooking pot and ladle

Slowly heat the pot and add ghee. Heat until the ghee begins to boil and add cumin seeds. Cook until it turns dark brown. Then add the water. When the water boils, add the rice. Cook for 10 to 15 minutes. As the water slowly evaporates, slow the fire and put the lid on the cooking pot for five minutes. Then it will be ready to serve. It is a good match for any curries. Serve with a red wine, such as pinot noir.

Benefits include high mineral content and fiber, carbohydrates with low calories. We eat this dish mostly at parties and festivals.

KHAJA [Buckwheat Bread]

Snack

Phapar Ko Roti

Everyone who lives in the Himalayas eats four times a day. The snack between lunch and dinner is khaja. The food we use for the snack can be seasonal, like boiled potato in the summer, popcorn and beans in the winter, or buckwheat bread, soup and beaten rice, which can be prepared in any season. Organic buckwheat flour and barley wheat are available at any natural food store.

This recipe for phapar ko roti will serve four people.

20 oz. buckwheat flour

1 ½ liters of water

3 tablespoons of olive oil or ghee

3 liters of tumba (fermented millet beer) or buttermilk

Frying pan and ladle

Immerse the flour in the water for 20 minutes. This makes the dough, which should be mushy. Heat a large iron frying pan and put in a little olive oil. When the pan is hot, put in one ounce of the buckwheat dough. Spread the dough evenly on the pan and cook with a slow heat for three minutes before turning it over. Cook the other side for another three minutes with the lid on the frying pan. It should be served with tumba for the adults and with buttermilk for children.

Benefits include 97% of the magnesium and 19% of the iron we require. This food is high in protein and the minerals are good for your heart and brain. It is gluten-free.

GAHU KO BHAT   [Wheat Rice]

Wheat rice

Wheat plants in the Himalayas are pure, green and healthy. Fields are vibrant, verdant, shiny green. Bugs cannot survive in the Himalayas. Wheat has a strong aroma with a high character. We grind it in a stone mill, first into pieces, then into flour. We make bhat from large pieces of wheat and flour makes the bread.

This recipe for gahu ko bhat will serve three people:

16 oz. coarsely ground wheat, immersed in water for 10 minutes.

1 liter of water

2 tablespoons of yak ghee

¼ teaspoon of fenugreek

1 medium-sized cooking pot

Heat the cooking pot and add the ghee. Continue to heat it until it boils, then add the fenugreek. Cook until it is dark brown in color. Then add the water and heat until boiling. Add the coarsely ground wheat. Cook for 10 minutes and stir with a ladle. Put the lid on the pot and wait for four minutes until it is ready to serve. Garnish it with vegetable curry and serve it with red wine.

Benefits from this meal include 651 calories per cup, 20% iron, 45% carbohydrates, 23% potassium. It is high in minerals, such as phosphorus and copper, and in folates.

GAHUKO ROTI [Wheat Bread]

Wheat bread

Non-processed bread cooked with non-processed wheat flour. This bread is made without any baking powder or baking soda. Cooked this way brings out the real taste of the wheat, its natural flavor and aroma.

This recipe for gahuko roti is meant to serve two people.

8 oz. of wheat flour

12 oz. of water

4 teaspoons purified buffalo butter (ghee)

A pinch of salt

In a large, round pan, combine the flour, salt and water to make a mush and wait for ten minutes.

Heat frying pan and add ghee. When it smells fragrant, add one ounce of wheat mush and spread it around on the bottom of the pan. Cook it for two minutes over a medium fire, then turn it over and cook it with the lid on the pan for another three minutes. When it is ready there will be such a delicious aroma you will smell it in your soul and your brain.

Serve this with chutney and eat it with milk or wine.

Health benefits: strengthens the bones so you can work harder. This is an international favorite cuisine prepared in different ways.

DAL KO TARKARY [Lentil Curry]

Lentil Curry

Dal ko tarkary is a curry of lentils. It can be a soup or mush. Cook with spices for higher flavor.   This recipe will serve three people.

10 oz. red lentils (musari dal) immersed in water for 30 minutes

1 liter of water

2 tablespoons olive oil

1 onion finely chopped

1 tomato finely chopped

2 tablespoons of chopped garlic

3 tablespoons of chopped ginger

10 coriander seeds

10 pieces of cumin seed

½ teaspoon garam masala

¼ teaspoon turmeric

¼ teaspoon paprika

½ teaspoon salt

½ teaspoon red chili powder

¼ cup chopped cilantro

¼ of a lime

Medium cooking pot and ladle

Heat oil, add cumin and coriander seed, and cook until seeds release oil and aroma. Add onion, stir and cook until light brown. Then add garlic and ginger, and cook until brown. Add tomato and cook for two more minutes. Then you add everything else except the water, lime and cilantro. Cook for two minutes and then add water. Cook five more minutes and when the water is absorbed, the mixture will get juicy. Reduce heat. Then add the cilantro and lime. Taste before serving.

Health benefits: contains enough fiber and protein. You can eat it with rice to increase calories for hard-working people. The spices, like garlic, ginger, onions and turmeric, impart anti-cancer properties.

If you cook black lentils or black garbanzo beans you must cook for a longer time.

MISAYARA BHUTEKO TARKARI [Vegetable Sauté]

Mixed vegetable sauté

Misayara bhuteko tarkari is a mixed vegetable sauté with salt and spices. Eat as an appetizer for a vegetarian complement to your drinks with guests. Mixing more than seven vegetables is better for your nutrient values.

Misayara bhuteko tarkari (serves four people)

1 potato cut into ½ inch thin slices as big as your finger in size

1 carrot (medium) cut into bite-sized pieces

½ cabbage cut into 1 inch squares

½ onion chopped same size as the cabbage

4 black mushrooms chopped into 2 inch pieces

1 oz. broccoli cut into 1 inch pieces

1 oz. bok choy chopped into half-finger sized pieces

2 tablespoons olive oil

¼ tablespoon salt

¼ teaspoon red chili powder

¼ teaspoon coriander seeds

¼ teaspoon cumin seeds

¼ teaspoon fenugreek seeds

¼ teaspoon paprika

¼ teaspoon turmeric

½ lime

A large, non-stick open pot or frying pan

Heat the pot or frying pan with the oil. Add cumin and coriander seeds, and then cook until brown. Add fenugreek seeds and cook until they release oil and a fragrant aroma. Add potato, cook for two minutes. Then add the carrots, cook two more minutes and add all the vegetables. Cook for two more minutes at high heat. Then add the spices and salt. Cook for six minutes, add the lime juice and serve.

Benefits: contains phytochemicals, protein, and is rich in calcium. Contains all the vitamins except for vitamin B.

SABJIHARUKO KHOLE [Vegetable Soup]

Vegetable Soup

Sabjiharuko khole is good for sick people as well as healthy people. Sick people can't eat hard food. It is also good for everyone to heal their bodies, especially in the winter. It contains more than seven different vegetables, more healing properties for your internal organs.

This recipe will serve four people.

1 medium potato, chopped into small pieces

1 carrot (2 oz.) chopped very small

½ oz. green beans, chopped small

1 onion chopped finely

1 oz. broccoli, chopped small

1 oz. cauliflower, chopped small

1 whole red bell pepper, chopped small

1 tablespoon ground garlic

2 tablespoons ground ginger

2 tablespoons olive oil

½ tablespoon salt

½ teaspoon red chili powder

½ tablespoon garam masala

½ teaspoon turmeric

½ teaspoon paprika

½ teaspoon ajwan

¼ cup cilantro, finely chopped

½ lime

1 ½ liters of water

One cooking pot and ladle

Heat pot with oil, add ajwan and cook until dark brown and the aroma can be smelled. Add onion and potato together cooking for four minutes, and add the carrots, bell pepper and green beans. Cook for four more minutes. Then add the cauliflower and the broccoli and cook for three minutes. Add the salt, chili powder and the other spices except the lime, cilantro and water. Cook for two more minutes. Add the water. Cook until the vegetables release their fats and become liquid. Add cilantro and lime by squeezing the juice. Taste before taking it off the fire.

The health benefits include being good for people sick in bed with all the plant minerals which nurture the body and mind. This lets us heal better. It is really good in winter to warm your body if you add more spices.

SAG SABJIHARUKO TARKARI [Vegetable Curry]

Mixed Vegetable Curry

Sag sabjiharuko tarkari is very popular in the Himalayas. It is grown on their farms. Everything is fresh, clean and safe. They ferment the vegetables and save them for winter. Gundruk (fermented radish leaves) and sinki (smashed and dried radish root) are very popular winter dishes to warm your body.

Sag sabjiharuko tarkari to serve three people:

1 potato, cut into bite-sized pieces

1 onion, finely chopped

2 tomatoes, cut into small pieces

¼ eggplant, cut into small pieces

4 okras, cut into small pieces

2 carrots, cut small

5 mushrooms cut into halves

1 oz. spinach

2 tablespoons olive oil

½ tablespoon salt

3 tablespoons of chopped ginger

1 tablespoon of ground garlic

½ teaspoon black sesame seeds

½ teaspoon white sesame seeds

½ teaspoon red chili powder

½ tablespoon garam masala

½ teaspoon turmeric

½ teaspoon paprika

½ oz. oregano

½ lime

¼ cup cilantro

1 liter of water

One large open pot and ladle

Heat a large pot with olive oil and add the white and black sesame seeds. Cook until you smell the aroma. Add the onion and cook until light brown. Then add the potato, garlic and ginger. Cook for three minutes and then add the tomato, eggplant, okra, carrots and mushrooms. Cook for five minutes on high heat. Add salt and everything else except the lime, cilantro and water. Cook for three more minutes until the vegetables get soft and turn to mush, then add the water. Cook for ten minutes, then add the cilantro and lime. Taste before serving. Good with rice or bread.

Benefits: Contains many vitamins except vitamin-B. Low in calories, high in nutrients. Makes you feel light, clean and fresh in your body.

SISHNU KO TARKARI [Nettles Curry]

Nettles Curry

Nettles is a plant that can sting. You must handle it carefully. The leaves can be dried to make tea and a powder for making curry. When cooked it is very tasty.

Sishnu ko tarkari (green nettles curry) to serve three people:

3 cups of nettle leaves or buds

1 tablespoon ground garlic

2 cups of water

½ teaspoon of salt

½ teaspoon red chili powder

A medium-sized cooking pot and a ladle with chopping fins.

Heat the pot with water, add nettles and stir them until they are completely cooked (about 5 minutes). Add garlic, salt and chili powder. Chop by spinning the ladle between your palms. It will turn into a thick liquid. Taste before you serve. Good with rice, bread or dhero (millet mash).

Health benefits: contains vitamin B-6 and Vitamin A, which have many healing properties including for eyes and bones. This is a curry everybody needs to try.

KUKHURAKO BHUTEKO MASU [Chicken Sauté]

Chicken Sauté

Local free-ranging roosters from the Himalayas are so active and healthy that they are very tasty. It is good to have as an appetizer with your good friends and family.

Chicken Sauté to serve five people:

1 medium-sized rooster, cut into small pieces with the bones

3 onions, chopped finely

1 green onion leaf, finely chopped

2 tomatoes, chopped into small pieces

4 tablespoons mustard oil

4 tablespoons ground ginger

3 tablespoons ground garlic

3 tablespoons cumin seeds, immersed in water for 15 minutes, then strained and stone-ground

½ teaspoon turmeric

½ teaspoon paprika

½ tablespoon salt

½ teaspoon red chili powder

2 ½ liters of water

½ nutmeg, ground

½ teaspoon Asaphotida

1 large iron pot and ladle

Heat the pot with oil, add onion and cook until light brown. Then add garlic and ginger. Cook until golden brown over a slow heat. Add the chicken with the bones. Cook for 10 minutes while stirring. Add everything except the water, cumin and onion leaves. Cook for 5 minutes. Add water. Cook for 45 minutes over high heat. Burn chicken feathers and grind to powder to add in the middle of the cooking process. Add green onion leaves and ground cumin. Cook until water is absorbed by the meat to become a sauté. If the meat is old, cooking will take longer. Taste before serving. This is good served with red wine.

Health benefits: You get the active character from the rooster's spirit with moderate calories and high calcium, which helps your bones grow bigger and stronger. Your bone marrow produces blood. More blood is good for more energy and stamina.

KUKHURAKO MASUKO TARKARI [Chicken Curry]

Chicken Curry

Local free-range chicken is best for clean energy to succeed at any battle tomorrow. Chicken curry, good to be eaten with rice, theple bhat, bread, buckwheat mess. This recipe can also be used to cook different kinds of meat.

Kukhurako masuko tarkari cooked to serve five people:

1 chicken cut into small pieces with the bones

4 tablespoons olive oil

½ tablespoon salt

½ teaspoon red chili powder

3 onions finely chopped

3 tomatoes chopped

¼ teaspoon cumin seeds

¼ teaspoon coriander seeds

¼ teaspoon fenugreek

3 tablespoons crushed garlic

4 tablespoons chopped ginger

1 teaspoon turmeric

1 teaspoon paprika

½ tablespoon garam masala

3 tablespoons cumin seeds, soaked in water and then stone-ground

¼ cup chopped dill

½ lime

3 liters of water

1 large open iron pot and ladle

Heat the pot and olive oil, add cumin and coriander seeds and cook to light brown. Add fenugreek seeds and cook over a slow fire until lightly smoking. Then add onion and cook until golden brown. Add chicken, and stir periodically for ten minutes. Then add everything but the water, lime and dill. Cook for 10 minutes. Then add water and cook for 45 minutes in high heat. Add ground cumin, cook for 4 more minutes. Add dill and lime. When it has been cooked, the meat has to be with the gravy. Meat with the gravy is called a curry. We can mix the curry with the rice to eat. In Nepalese culture rice is a male food and curry is a female food. In Nepal cuisine has to have a rice and curry. Taste before serving. Can be served with zinfandel.

Health benefits: contains medium calories for people who work hard during the day or night. You get almost complete nutrition and vitamins. Good for raising the energy of sick people as well as everybody.

YAK KO MASUKO TARKARI [Yak Curry]

Yak Curry

The yak is a very curious animal. It is only found in the high Himalayan Mountains. They have long horns and long, bushy hair. Yaks eat foods consisting mostly of herbs and medicinal plants. Yak meat and blood are medicinal, with high levels of Omega-3. It is one of the best meats in the world. It is better than fish. Everybody has to see and learn of the yak.

Yak ko masuko tarkari

Yak curry, prepared to serve four people:

2 lbs. yak meat cut into small pieces, including the bones

2 onions, finely chopped

2 tomatoes, chopped

2 tablespoons mustard oil

½ tablespoon salt

20 cumin seeds

20 coriander seeds

20 fenugreek seeds

1 teaspoon garam masala

½ teaspoon paprika

½ teaspoon chili powder

½ teaspoon turmeric

2 ½ liters of water

¼ cup of cilantro, finely chopped

Big iron pot and ladle

Heat oil in the pot and add cumin and coriander seeds. Cook until light brown. Add fenugreek seeds. When the oils have been released it will give off an aroma. Add the chopped onion and cook until light brown. Then add yak meat and stir periodically for five minutes. Cook for two minutes and then add everything else but the cilantro and water. Cook for four minutes, then add water. Cook for 45 minutes at high heat and then add the cilantro. It must be saucy to go with the rice. Taste before serving. It is good with basmati rice and Zinfandel red wine, or tin pane rakshi.

Health benefits: Omega-3 is good for the heart and brain. Low calorie meat doesn't make you fat. Your body feels like a Sherpa. You will feel green, clean, fresh and enlightening.

BADELKO POLEKO MASU [Boar BBQ]

Boar Barbecue

In Nepal there are wild pigs. Not many people risk the danger to hunt wild boars but if they get lucky, the barbecued boar is very tasty. If you know how to use spices, that will increase the taste unbelievably. This recipe can be used to cook other kinds of meat except fish.

Badelko Poleko Masu

Wild boar barbecue, to serve five people

5 lbs. of boar meat with the skin, boar chops and ribs

4 tablespoons ground garlic

6 tablespoons ground ginger

2 tablespoons paprika

2 tablespoons garam masala

1 tablespoon turmeric

1 tablespoon chili powder

2 tablespoons soy sauce

4 tablespoons mustard oil

1 tablespoon salt

1 cup plain yoghurt

A barbecue oven or clay oven

Charcoal

Long tongs

Matches

Large bowl

Large tray

Gloves

Put the boar ribs and chopped meat into the large bowl. Then add everything. Mix thoroughly, and leave it overnight. Fire the oven. Heat it with charcoal. When the charcoal has burned down halfway at low heat, put the meat in the oven for five minutes. Turn it over and keep it cooking while checking the low fire. Turn the meat whenever necessary and cut it to check it inside. When it is soft, juicy and brown it will be done. Taste before you serve. Eat it with your favorite drinks and a salad, pickles, bread or rice.

Health benefits: medium in calories, with vitamin B, high in calcium and very juicy. It will make you very strong.

KHIR [Rice Pudding]

Rice Pudding

Khir is a dessert. It is high in calories and satisfies your brain. Diabetic people should avoid rice pudding.

This recipe is enough to serve two:

1 ½ ounces of rice, immersed in water to 30 minutes.

1 liter whole milk

¼ teaspoon cardamom seeds

5 cloves

¼ teaspoon rose water

3 tablespoons sugar or honey

A medium-sized pot and ladle

Heat the milk in the pot and add the rice when the milk begins to boil. Cook while stirring for five minutes and then add everything except the rosewater and sugar. Cook over low heat for fifteen minutes and then add the sugar. Stir gently for two minutes, then add the rosewater. Taste before serving.

Health benefits: high carbohydrates are good for filling all 5 trillion of the cells in your body. It has enough calcium and proteins, and contains vitamin D from the milk.

CHISO KERA [Icy Banana]

Icy Banana

Chiso kera is a dessert. Servings for two:

Take one banana and put it in a freezer for two hours

½ oz. beaten rice*, lightly fried to brown

Peel the banana and chop into small pieces. Mix with the beaten rice. Enjoy the dessert.

Health benefits: medium calories in a cold, sweet banana eaten with crunchy, beaten rice. Good for your teeth. Bananas contain potassium and phosphorus, which are good for your eyes.

You can use this recipe to prepare manila mango and sweet apples.

*Beaten rice: Take cooked rice, put in in a bow and mash it with a pestle until flat.

CHAI [Aromatic Tea]

Spice Tea

Chai is a bud picked from a plant. It is dried in the sun. We cook chai with extra spices in order to increase the taste and aroma, to give the tea extra character. We drink tea for all occasions, especially on special occasions. Offer chai to any guests who visit you.

Chai, spice tea, recipe for serving two people:

½ tablespoon ground Ilame or Darjeeling tea

½ size of your finger scrubbed ginger

4 cloves

4 cardamoms, broken up

¼ teaspoon ground cinnamon

4 ounces of milk

1 ½ liter of water

1 tablespoon brown sugar or honey

Kettle and strainer

Boil the water and add milk and chai. Cook for five minutes. Then add cardamom, cinnamon and cloves. Cook for ten minutes at high heat. Add ginger. Cook for four more minutes until ready to serve. Use the filter to strain the tea. Use honey or sugar to sweeten for your desired taste.

Health benefits: spicy, aromatic chai will set your mood and raise energy for positive work. Contains mineral liquids and vitamins.

GUNDRUK KO JHOL [National Soup]

Gundruk Soup

National soup of Nepal

Gundruk consists of fermented radish leaves. It is a good deterrent against winter colds. It is customary to offer it to guests. Gundruk can be cooked as a curry, chutney or soup.

Recipe for four people:

4 oz. of gundruk immersed in water for 30 minutes

2 tablespoons mustard oil

½ tablespoon salt

1 finely chopped onion

1 chopped tomato

½ teaspoon hot chili powder

1 green onion leaf finely chopped

1 tablespoon ground garlic

2 tablespoons ground ginger

½ teaspoon paprika

½ teaspoon turmeric

¼ teaspoon ground timbur (sichuan pepper)

½ teaspoon ajwan

2 liters of water

½ lime

Medium pot and ladle

Heat the pot with the oil in it and add ajwan when the oil is hot. Cook until the aroma is released. The fragrance will ignite your senses and desire to cook. Add onion and cook until it turns light brown. Then add garlic and ginger. Cook until golden brown. Add tomato and salt. Cook for four more minutes. It will become tadka, an aromatic gravy. Add gundruk and cook for five more minutes. Then add paprika, turmeric, chili powder and cook for two more minutes. Add water. Boil for 20 minutes at high heat. Add onion leaf, timbur and lime. Cook for two minutes and taste before serving.

Health benefits: this is a super-flavored soup. It is perfect with a high character from Sagarmatha, which means "The Head of the World." It contains copper and vitamin B-6, which helps digestion.

EATING DISCIPLINE

People are working hard to manage their finance and families. They do not have enough time to prepare food, cook and enjoy their meals. Most people are depressed and reactive because they do not have eating discipline. They have many health problems like gastric disorders, diabetes, and migraine headaches. This includes aggressive behavior as well. You can be healthy by developing eating discipline.

Eat five times a day to fill your stomach with nutritional, low-calorie foods which will give you all the vitamins and minerals you need.

Stomach diagrams:

#1

4 ounces of steak and 1 tablespoon of olive oil

520 calories

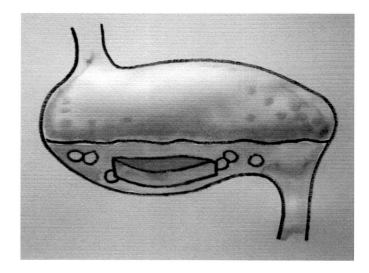

Picture #1: one teaspoon of olive oil and four ounces of beef contains 520 calories. You cannot fill your stomach with this amount of food. An empty stomach can cause gastric problems.

#2

Hamburger and French fries

1,200 calories

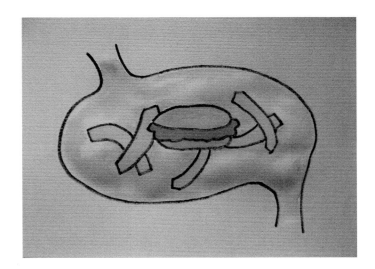

Picture #2: three tablespoons of frying oil contains almost 400 calories. Four ounces of beef contains 500 calories. One serving of French-fried potatoes contains almost 300 calories. Too many calories produce fat. People who suffer from obesity are getting less nutrition from their food.

#3

4 ounces of fish, vegetables and fruits

Nuts and seeds 415 calories

Picture #3: one half pound of vegetables contains about 60 calories. Four ounces of fish contains about 200 calories. One apple is about 50 calories. One half ounce of walnuts has about 50 calories. One-half tablespoon of flax seeds contains 25 calories. One half tablespoon of sunflower seeds contains 30 calories.

The first picture shows food that is high in calories but not nutrition. When 75% of the stomach is empty you could have gastric and other problems. The second picture shows food with too many calories. This leads to obesity and other problems, including cancer and heart disease. Picture three shows a balanced diet with the right amount of calories and good nutrition.

A balanced diet can give you the perfect shape, size, and health of your body.

Hard-working people require 2,000 calories per day. You can receive this amount with the following foods:

Grains: 6 0z. per day

Vegetables: 2 ½ cups daily

Fruits: 2 cups

Oil: 6 teaspoons daily

Meat and beans: 5 ½ ounces daily

FAST METABOLISM AND SLOW METABOLISM

People with a fast metabolism digest their food faster and turn it into calories. They are active and strong, and they are not fat. They eat more food and eat it more often. They are lucky their systems work well and fast.

People with slow metabolisms eat slowly and digest food slowly. This makes them heavy. It takes longer to turn food into calories and this converts to fat. They tend to be slow-working. They generally don't realize the cause of their weight problems. People must learn their metabolic rates and control their weight.

Protein is hard to digest. It is obtained from meat, eggs, seeds and dairy products. Pepsin is the chemical that breaks down the food containing protein. The processes of digestion are metabolic and catabolic. Food can take from 24 to 72 hours to digest. The human digestive tract is 9 meters long. Elderly people and children have less digestive power than adults. Eating vegetables, sweets, fats and liquids digest faster than protein.

People eat too much cheese and fried foods. Over time this turns into a habit. High-calorie foods with fat and too much cholesterol will plug up the arteries in your heart. Your habit will become a problem. This is called habit of the habit, pain of the pain. Use your intelligence to choose what foods to eat and consider how long digestion will take.

RDA [Recommended Daily Allowance]

RDA for a balanced diet

What is the RDA? It is the Recommended Daily Allowance. The RDA was established during the Second World War for the nutritional needs of the soldiers. RDA tells you how many calories you need for a day for different kinds of work. Various parts of the body need different kinds of food in different amounts. No single food works for all parts of the body.   Since then many doctors and scientists have reviewed the RDA for public health.

Many people have health problems from consuming mostly meat and dairy products. This causes heart attacks and obesity.

Scientists researched these health problems all over the world. They found that eating more fruits and vegetables than meat and dairy foods is the way to avoid health problems. They learned in the China Project that eating a diet consisting of 90% vegetables keeps you very healthy and slim.

In Nepal we eat a diet of 70% vegetables and the people there are very healthy and not obese. The scientists discovered the RDA for all of our nutritional needs. Normal people need 200 to 800 calories per day for housework. People working in offices need 1,500 calories if they are men and 1,300 calories if they are women. Hard working men and pregnant women need 2,000 calories.

The RDA for different bodily needs: 50 grams of protein for adult men and 1,500 milligrams of calcium, 10,000 International Units of vitamin-A, 1.5 milligrams of vitamin-B, 1,200 milligrams of vitamin-C, 500 I.U. of vitamin-D, and 200 I.U. of vitamin-E. Fat: 20%. Carbohydrates: 325 grams. Iron: 8 milligrams ordinarily, with 18 mg. for women during pregnancy or menstruation. Omega-3: 1.29 grams.

It is always good to maintain the RDA from the womb to young child and on to old age.

[Source: individual numbers garnered from https://www.nal.usda.gov/fnic/dietary-reference-intakes and other related sites]

RDA FOR DIFFERENT NEEDS OF THE BODY

Protein: We get protein from meat, dairy, vegetables, grains, seeds and nuts. Eating 50% vegetables and two fruits a day will give you enough protein to reach your RDA. Protein is good for the growth of the cells of your body. Eating meat and dairy products give you more protein. Excessive protein causes health problems like cardiac conditions and cancer. Fruits and vegetables containing plant proteins are better for your health.

Calcium: This is a mineral that helps to make your bones healthy and bigger. You obtain calcium from meat, dairy foods and vegetables. It is contained in bok choy, turnips, collard greens, tofu, kale, romaine lettuce, carrots and milk. These foods have the most calcium. Consuming too much or too little calcium can cause health problems. Vegetable calcium is better for your health than meat or dairy calcium.

Vitamin-A: This is good for your eyes and brain. You can get it from nettles, kale, mustard greens, Swiss chard, red or green chili peppers, butter squash, pumpkins, papayas, mangos and carrots. Your eyes work more than your other organs. You need enough vitamin-A, otherwise you might go blind.

B-vitamins: there are eight forms of vitamin B. These vitamins are good for your bones and digestive system. You can obtain these vitamins from meat, fish and nettles. Vegetarians do not get enough B-vitamins, so they need to take supplements.

Vitamin-C: This is good for skin and cells. It is a liquid. It nourishes your skin and keeps you young. It is contained in red and green chili peppers, broccoli, kale, water cress, green beans, cabbage, strawberries, fruits and vegetables.

Vitamin-D: This is good for bones and circulation. We can get vitamin-D from mushrooms, milk and sunshine. Sitting in the sun for 12 minutes is good for your skin. Not enough vitamin-D causes osteoporosis.

Vitamin-E: This heals your body and moisturizes your skin and hair. Almonds, papayas, pistachios and walnuts contain vitamin-E.

Vitamin-K: This dissolves blood clots. It is found in papayas, green leafy vegetables and walnuts.

Iron: This is a blood booster. It can be obtained from yak, bison, venison, beef and spinach. Iron make blood cells red, which carries oxygen to the rest of the body. Many people are iron deficient. That makes them weak and tired.

Fats: Fats come in two types, saturated and unsaturated. Fats are derived from animals, dairy products and oils from vegetables, nuts, grains and fruits.

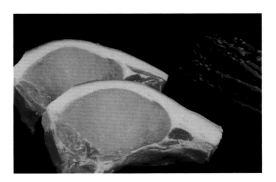

Carbohydrates: These convert into glucose which yields energy. There are two types of carbohydrates. Refined carbohydrates have no nutrition. Unrefined carbohydrates have nutrients. Carbohydrates are contained in potatoes, radishes, grains and beans.

Omega 3: This is a fatty acid. It is known as a brain food. It helps heart and blood vessels of the brain. It is obtained from flax seed, walnuts, soy beans, salmon, garlic and turmeric.

Omega-3 foods include:

Flax seed (one tablespoon) contains 1.7 grams

Walnuts (four tablespoons) contains 2 grams

Soybeans (one-half cup) 2 grams

Tofu (one and one-half cups) 2 grams

Salmon, bison and yak meat also have omega-3 nutrients. Consume 1-2 grams of omega-3 daily. This will prevent heart disease, diabetes and chronic diseases. Omega-3 also helps your brain and your heart.

Omega-6: This is produced by our bodies. It is also found in dairy, meat, fowl and eggs. If you consume more than you need, it raises blood pressure and leads to depression, inflammation and other sicknesses.

CONTROL AND CURE FOR DIABETES

There are two types of diabetes, Type One and Type Two. Rising sugar levels in the blood is what we call diabetes. Eating sweet fats and carbohydrates will make sugar levels rise and this can cause death. Eating a low sugar level diet is also dangerous to your health. Diabetics can control sugar through their diet. Normal, healthy people do not need to control their blood sugar level. It is regulated automatically by your body.

Diabetes is caused by genetics, not following the RDA, eating too many calories and not getting enough exercise. Diabetes can be controlled by eating fewer carbs, less fat, sugar and sweets. Instead, eat fruits, vegetables, nuts and grains. Vegan food is good for diabetes. Vegans do not eat meat, eggs or dairy foods. Recommended to be eaten are wild rice, green vegetables, fruits and salads.

You can try this diet for three months to cure diabetes. Combine these foods with exercise and stay

healthy.

1 cup of wild rice is 166 calories

1 cup of lentil soup is 100 calories

1 cup of salad is 50 calories

1 cup of steamed vegetables is 50 calories

Total = 366 calories

1 lb of salad is about 100 calories.

HOW TO LOSE WEIGHT

Weight gain is a complicated process. It can be genetic, dietary, or caused by hormones, lack of physical exercise and stress. Eating more calories than you burn causes you to get fat.

People with slow metabolic rates have difficulty controlling their weight. Research has discovered that weight can be controlled. Eating high-calorie foods such as meat, cheese, nuts, cakes, fried foods and refined-flour pizza or pastries loaded with sugar causes obesity. It is very difficult to lose weight. You must measure your food calories and the nutritional value of the food before you eat.

Non-exercise Activity Thermogenesis (NEAT) takes in normal housework like cooking, cleaning and gardening. Light work burns from 200 to 800 calories per day. Work in an office (medium physical work) uses up 1,500 calories in men and 1,300 calories in women per day. Hard-working people who require a lot of exercise burn 2,000 calories per day. How many calories do you need to climb Mount Everest in ten hours? Take a guess.

Eating low-calorie fruits and vegetables and less caloric grain with high nutritional value will cause you to lose weight. There are two ways to lose weight. First, eat only enough calories in your food to burn for one day. Second, you can consume more calories but you must burn them up with exercise. If you do not burn up your intake of calories you will get fat and unhealthy. It is good to eat foods rich in iron at least once a week to boost your energy. High-calorie fruits and vegetables like bananas, potatoes, radishes and sweet fruits are to be avoided.

Research conducted on fruits and vegetables shows that they have the power to protect the body from cancer, especially if eaten raw. Cooking destroys 60% of the phytochemicals. Eating salad will give you enough phytochemicals and will help you lose weight. If you are overweight eat more salads and soup to fill your stomach because it is very low in calories. It is good for your kidneys, health and beauty. Salad keeps your skin silky, fresh and glowing. You will look like an angel.

Eating 70% non-starchy vegetables, 20% low-calorie grains and 10% fruits and salads will definitely make you lose weight, maintain your RDA and fulfill your stomach.

NUTRITION IN FOOD AND DRINKS

PROPERTIES OF VEGETABLES

Green vegetables consist of about half protein, one quarter carbohydrates and a quarter fats. They also contain minerals and vitamins. Protein helps grow the body and carbohydrates give the body energy. Minerals maintain organs and bones. Liquids contained in vegetables help the system flow smoothly.

Nepalese farmers grow organic vegetables and also harvest wild vegetables like nettles and mushrooms. They harvest only when the vegetables are mature.

Eating chicken and bread is not as healthy as eating vegetables and grains. Eating vegetables increases strength and longevity.

Potatoes have more carbohydrates than the other vegetables. This gives the body more energy. Potatoes are very popular in Nepal as well as the rest of the world. Potatoes from the Himalayas are double the taste than those grown in the lower elevations in Nepal. They are twice as expensive.

Spinach is high in iron, a blood-booster. Many people throughout the world are deficient in iron. Broccoli has more protein than any other vegetable. Romaine lettuce makes a very good salad, especially if combined with radishes and spinach. Vegetables that are the color red, like red bell peppers, carrots, red chard and spinach are good for the eyes.

One pound of non-starchy vegetables has about 100 calories. Starchy vegetables contain more calories. Vegetables have more vitamins and minerals than meat. Meat has more calories and vitamin-B, iron and calcium from the bone and its marrow. Eating meat will not give you vitamins A, C, D, E nor K, nor will it give you magnesium nor potassium. Most animals eat plants. This keeps them healthy and strong. People learned to eat vegetables from the animals, learned to eat grain from the birds and learned to eat nuts from the squirrels. Vegetables and fruits are the true nectar of the gods. Kale has a greater variety of vitamins than other vegetables.

Vegetables are best in vitamins A and C, and in phytochemicals.

Nutrition for 100 calories of the following foods						
	Radish	Broccoli	Spinach	Kale	Potato	Romaine Lettuce
Carbohydrate	18 g	6.2 g	4 g	5 g	22 g	7 g
Protein	.60 g	8 g	3.10 g	6 g		6 g
Fat	4 g	.3 g	.4 g	0 g		0 g
Cholesterol	0 g	Low	0 g	0 g	0 g	0 g
Fiber	9 g	2.4 g	2.4 g	7.1 g	2 g	12 g
Zinc	.18 mg	1.1 mg	.8 mg	.8 mg		.3 mg
Folates	154 mcg	190 mcg	2.5 mcg	45 mcg		805 mcg
Niacin	16 mg	1.5 mg	.8 mg	1.6 mg		1.6 mg
Riboflavin	.038 mg	25 mg		.22 mg		4 mg
Vitamin A	45 IU		8,315 IU	46,000 IU		50,200 mcg
Vitamin C	86.6 mg	140 mg	32.10 mg	143 mg	20 mg	140 IU
Vitamin E		4.5 mg	2.4 mg	2.9 mg		7.1 mg
Potassium	.1450 mg	501 mg	460 mg	812 mg	600 mg	1.45 mg
Magnesium	59.5 mg	40 mg	102 mg	62 mg		80 mg
Beta Carotene	.5 mg	2.1 mg		28.150 mcg		30.705 mcg
Iron	.23 mg	2.1 mg	3.1 mg	3.1 mg	1.2 mg	.7 mg
Calcium	225 mg	115 mg	110 mg	245 mg	19 mg	8 mg

PROPERTIES OF FRUITS

Avocados are high in calories, fats and carbohydrates. It can be made into oil, chips and salads. Avocados are the most expensive fruits in the world. They are easy to digest.

Apples, oranges and mangos are high in vitamins and minerals. There are many kinds of apples with many different flavors. There are many types of oranges. Some are red and some are yellow. There are many types of mangos. Manila mangos are the most expensive. They come from South America and the tropical countries. Mangos are very good for your eyes.

Kiwi, papaya, plums, cranberries, blackberries, persimmons and strawberries are high in vitamin-C and many minerals. There are many different types of persimmons. Some can be eaten right from the tree and some must be eaten a week after being picked.

Grapes can be eaten or made into wine. They are high in vitamin-C and minerals. There are two colors of grapes and many different kinds. Green grapes are best when picked a month sooner than red grapes. Red wine has more alcohol than white wine. The older vines produce the best grapes. That is why grapes from older vines have a stronger flavor than grapes from younger vines. One glass of red wine every day is good for your health.

Fruits from the top branches of the trees are always more ripe because they receive more sunshine and produce more vitamin-D.

Fruits and nuts are good to eat anytime and anywhere, especially on long travels. They are easy to carry and are a good source of energy. When people of Nepal go on hikes of several days they carry fruits, nuts and sautéed grains. Nuts and grains can be ground into a powder for very young children and elderly people to avoid being chewed. You must eat two to four fruits every day to complete your nutritional needs. Fruit can be cut into small slices and dried for future use.

One medium-sized apple contains 62 calories. One medium avocado has 320 calories. A medium-sized orange contains 60 calories. A banana has 105 calories. A strawberry had four calories. A papaya has 119 calories. A mango has 103 calories. A pear has 96 calories. A fig contains 37 calories. A plum has 30 calories. A persimmon has 50 calories and is high in carotene and lutein. One peach has 38 calories. One grape has 4 calories.

Eating fruit is better than drinking fruit juice because vitamins and minerals are destroyed during the blending. Fruits are best in vitamin A and vitamin C. Fruit also has carbohydrates for quick energy when you are hungry.

Nutrition in 100 grams of fruits							
Fruit	Fat	Calories	Carbohydrates	Iron	Protein	Vitamin C	Vitamin A
Apple	17 g	52	13.82 g	1%	0	17%	54.01 IU
Avocado	14.65 g	160	8.53 g	3%	2 g	17%	3%
Orange	.12 g	47	11.73 g	1%	.94 g	89%	4%
Banana	.33 g	89	22.84 g	1%	1.09 g	14%	1%
Blackberry	4.1 g	43	9.61 g	.6 mg	4.7 g	21.01 mg	214 IU
Strawberry	.3 g	32	11.67 g	2%	.67 mg	98%	0
Kiwi	.52 g	61	14.66 g	2%	1.94 g	54%	2%
Mango	.27 g	64	17 g	1%	.51 g	46%	15%
Papaya	.14 g	39	9.81 g	1%	.6 g	103%	22%
Pear	.12 g	58	15.46 g	1%	.39 g	7%	0
Fig	.39 g	74	19.18 g	2%	.75 g	3%	3%
Plum	.29 g	46	11.5 g	1%	.7 g	16%	7%
Persimmon	.19 g	70	18.57 g	.15 g	.58 g	7.5 mg	81 IU
Peach	.25 g	39	9.54 g	1%	.91 g	11%	7%
Grapes	.16 g	69	18.1 g	2%	.72 g	18%	
Cranberry	.13 g	46	12.2 g	1%	.3 g	22%	

PROPERTIES OF MEAT

Different kinds of meat have different properties. Deer, beef, bison and yak have the highest levels of iron. Iron is good for athletes. Salmon is good for students because omega-3 fatty acids will nurture their brains. Pork, chicken and lamb are good for a calorie boost. Pork is best in a barbecue because it has fat that turns crunchy and savory, especially with spices.

Yak is a very special animal. It is only raised in the high altitude of the Himalayas. Yak cattle are ten times more expensive than cow cattle. Yaks eat herbs and plants that are medicinal. Yak milk and meat are medicinal. People in Nepal believe it can cure cancer. The Nepalese eat old animals in bone soup to heal their body aches, especially aches in their joints. Free-ranging animals are more nutritious than animals raised in cages or pens. Fish acquire mercury from water pollution. Purchase these meats from reputable stores.

People who eat meat are sometimes more relaxed and happy. Meat helps our bodies to run smoothly. Iron rich meats are more expensive and important for athletes and pregnant women.

Nutrition in 100 grams per serving cooked						
Meat	Fat	Calories	Cholesterol	Vitamin B-12	Protein	Iron
Bison	2.42 g	143	82 mg	2.86 mcg	21.62 g	3.42 mg
Beef	10.15 g	219	86 mg	2.65 mcg	21.39 g	2.99 mg
Pork	9.66 g	212	86 mg	.75 mcg	19.74 g	1.1 mg
Chicken	7.41 g	190	89 mg	.33 mcg	18.6 g	1.21 mg
Salmon	10.97 g	216	87 mg	5.8 mcg	19 g	.55 mg
Yak	2 g	120	88 mg	2.85 mcg	23 g	15%
Lamb	10.15 g	219	88 mg	2.2 mcg	25 g	1.5 mg
Deer	4 g	265	0 mg	2.3 mcg	26.5 g	3.3 mg

PROPERTIES OF GRAINS

Brown rice and quinoa have more protein and minerals. Quinoa is a very popular grain. Millet is very good to eat and for making wine. If you go to Nepal, you must try the millet tumba and the tin pane rakshi. Tumba is fermented millet beer and tin pane rakshi is a traditional style of making wine.

Basmati rice, jasmine rice and wild rice are very nice in flavor. Buckwheat and wheat flour have lots of iron, which is good for blood. Yellow corn is unique in color and flavor, with many vitamins and minerals.

Eating too much grain can be a problem for diabetic people because it is high in carbohydrates. Grains are an energy food.

Nutrition in 100 grams of grains							
Grain	Calories	Fat	Carbohydrates	Protein	Fiber	Vitamin A	Iron
Basmati Rice	121	.038 mg	25.22 g	3.54 g	.4 g	0	7%
Brown Rice	360	3 mg	80%	10 g	32%	0	2.2 mg
Jasmine Rice	173	1 g	37 g	19 mg	0	0	0
Wild Rice cooked	101	.34 g	21.3 g	3.99 g	1.8 mg	0	3%
Quinoa cooked	120	17.6 g	85.1 g	4.4 g	2.8 mg	5 IU	1.5 mg
Yellow Corn	108	1.28 g	25.1 g	3.22 g	2.8 mg	5%	3%
White Corn	365	4.74 g	74.26 g	9.42 g	0		15%
Wheat Flour	339	1.9 g	72.6 g	13.7 g	12.2 g	9.1 IU	20%
Barley	354	2.3 g	73.48 g	12.48 g	13.3 g	0	20%
Buck Wheat	343	3.4 g	71.5 g	71.5 g	10 g	0	12%
Millet cooked	119	1 g	23.67 g	3.51 g	1.3 g	0	4%

PROPERTIES OF BEANS

There are more than 100 kinds of beans. Soy beans are highest in nutrition and fats. Soy beans are used to make tofu, soy milk and oil. They contain omega-3 fatty acids.

All beans are high in carbohydrates, fiber and proteins. People in South America eat lots of beans, which make them very strong.

There are two types of garbanzo beans, black and brown. They are very popular to eat.

There are two types of lentils, green and red.

Kidney beans, pinto beans, black-eyed beans and navy beans are high in iron. Cocoa beans are high in protein, fiber and calories. These beans are made into chocolate. Coffee beans are high in protein, fiber, iron and caffeine. Coffee beans make coffee. Too much coffee is dangerous for your health. Beans are best for fiber, which cleanses your rectum and colon.

Nutrition in 100 grams of beans							
Bean	Carbohydrates	Calories	Fat	Fiber	Protein	Vit. A	Iron
Garbanzo	60.65 g	164	2.6 g	7.6 g	8.9 g	270 IU	29 mg
Red Lentil	108 g	400	0	0	35 g	0	0
Green Lentil	60.01 g	353	9.5 g	14.9 g	25.8 g	39.0 IU	15%
Kidney	15.5 g	82	.6 g	4.3 g	5.22 g	0	6%
Soy	40.2 g	416	19.94 g	9.3 g	36.49 g		87%
Pinto	15.2 g	86	0	4.6 g	4.6 g	0	8%
Cocoa	55.1 g	228	13.7 g	37 g	19.6 g	0	13.86 mg
Blackeye Beans cooked	20.2 g	116	.5 g	6.5 g	7.7 g	15 IU	2.5 mg
Navy	25 g	113	.53 g	5.1 g	7.53 g	0	10%
Coffee Roasted	25.8 g	284	15.4 g	19.8 g	10.4 mg	0	23%

NUTRITION IN NUTS AND SEEDS

Nuts are high in nutrition and calories. Eating too many nuts can make you healthy and fat at the same time, but it is good fat. Fatty acid is omega-3, which helps smooth the blood flow in your heart and brain. Sunflower seeds, pumpkin seeds and all nuts have the same kind of nutrients. We can eat nuts and seeds with salad and use them in baking, roasting and cooking with curry and rice. I prefer to cook nuts and seeds with bread. Seeds and nuts can also make oil.

If you want to control your weight, eat less than 100 grams of seeds and nuts per day. They are also high in anti-cancer properties. One of my friends cured herself of cancer by eating lots of almonds.

Nuts and seeds are high in vitamin E and omega-3. In the Nepalese festival Tihar, sisters feed good food and seeds to their brothers to make them strong and to protect them.

Nutrition for 100 grams Nuts & Seeds						
Principal	Pistachio	Walnut	Almond	Peanuts	Cashew	Sunflower Seed
Calories	556 cal	650 cal	570 cal	567 cal	550 cal	570 cal
Carbohydrates	26.97 g	14.20 g	29.10 g	16.10 g	30.15 g	18.75 g
Protein	19.50 g	15.10 g	20.01 g	24.10 g	18.20 g	22.50 g
Fat	40.44 g	60.10 g	50.60 g	48.16 g	43.80 g	48.50 g
Cholesterol	0 mg	0 mg	0 mg	0 mg	30.19 g	0 mg
Fiber	10.2 g	6.9 g	11.10 g	8.4 g	3.2 g	10.4 g
Folates	50 pg	0 pg	44 pg	241 pg	25 pg	220 pg
Vitamin A	550 IU	.8 %	2 IU	0	0	50 IU
Vitamin C	4 mg	1%	0	0	.4 IU	1.3 IU
Calcium	105 mg	10%	2.6 mg	91 mg	34 mg	75 mg
Copper	1.5 mg	0	.99 mg	1.141 mg	2.154 mg	500 mg
Iron	4.1 mg	16%	3.71 mg	4.57 mg	6.67 mg	5 mg
Magnesium	120 mg	0	271 mg	165 mg	391 mg	300 mg
Zinc	2 mg	0	3.12 mg	0	4.5 mg	5 mg
Vitamin E	22.05 mg	0	26 mg	8.32 mg	5.30 mg	34.50 mg

PROPERTIES OF ROOTS

Turmeric:

Turmeric is a very popular spice throughout the world. It contains high levels of vitamins and minerals. In India and Nepal turmeric is used as a spice, as a medicine and for nutrition. It has antibacterial and anti-inflammatory properties. It can heal a cold and sore throat. Heat up water and add half a teaspoon of salt and turmeric, and then gargle five times until half of the glass has been used and drink the remaining mixture slowly.

Turmeric has three times more omega-3 than salmon. Turmeric is one of the most expensive roots among other roots and spices.

Ginger:

Ginger is also a spice and a medicine. Nepalese curry is not complete without ginger. It is a hot and upbeat spice. It helps alleviate nausea and queasiness. It can be brewed as a tea, added to food or eaten raw. It is high in vitamin C. Eating ginger every day can increase your health and happiness.

Garlic:

Garlic is a food, spice and medicine. Native Americans say it chases ghosts away. Putting garlic around your house keeps snakes away. In Nepalese cuisine garlic is essential as a spice to increase the flavor of the food. Garlic naan is more expensive than plain naan. Garlic has half as much omega-3 as salmon. Garlic is also an expensive root.

Onion:

Onion is a spice, food and medicine. It is so strong it will make you cry if eaten raw. In Nepal we use onion for healing pain, especially the pain of headaches. Onion can also help with cancer, blood pressure and diabetes. We can eat it raw, sautéed or made into a sauce. There are many different colors of onions. They can be red, brown or yellow.

Carrot and Sweet Potato:

Carrots and sweet potatoes are high in vitamin A. They are orange in color. They are good for your vision. You need vitamin A every day.

Yuca, Choyote, Potato, Yam, Yam Bean Jicama:

These are foods that are good for your health. You can eat them by steam-cooking or by grinding them into flour, flour mess or soup. Eating too much of these foods can make you gain weight.

Taro:

Taro is higher in vitamins and minerals than other roots. Taro leaves are also edible. We can find this in Nepal and South America. There are two types of taro. Small taro grows in Nepal. Large taro grows in South America.

Roots can be cut into slices and made into chips. They can be dried and ground into flour for future use. In Nepalese culture we eat roots once a year at a festival called Magheshakranti.

Roots are high in carbohydrates, almost like grains. Carbohydrates are good for energy.

Nutrition in 100 grams of Roots						
Root	Protein	Calories	Carbohydrates	Vitamin C	Fiber	Calcium
Tumeric	7.8 g	354	64.9 g	25 mg	21.1 g	183 mg
Ginger	1.82 g	80	17.77 g	8%	2 g	34 mg
Garlic	6.36 g	149	33.6 g	52%	2.1 g	18%
Onion	.92 gr	42	10.11 gr	11%	0	2%
Carrot*	1.19 g	52	12.26 g		3.6 g	4%
Yucca	1.4 g	160	38.1 g	13 IU	1.8 g	16 mg
Taro	.5 g	142	36.6 g	84.01 IU	5.1 g	18 mg
Potato	1.68 g	70	15.71 g	33%	0	1%
Yam	1.4 g	116	27.58 g	2%	3.9 g	1%
Sweet Potato*	1.57 g	86	20.12 g		3 g	3%
Yam Bean Jicama*	.72 g	38	8.82 g		4.9 g	1%

ALCOHOLIC BEVERAGES

Beer:

Beer is low in calories but high in carbohydrates. Consuming too much beer will make you drunk and fat. Consuming twelve ounces of beer in an hour will not make you drunk or fat.

Muscat:

Muscat is a sweet dessert wine. Drink only half as much as you would drink of red wine.

White Wine:

White wine is good in the hot summer to cool your body. You can warm up the cool wine to drink in the winter. The recipe for heated wine includes heating up a pot with oil and adding ajwan. Continue heating until the mixture turns dark brown. Put wine in the pot with honey and drink.

Red Wine:

Red wine is the best for health. It contains iron and has antioxidant properties. Drink one or two glasses before bedtime. It will be a healthy and beautiful night.

Black Label Whiskey:

This can be used as a medicine for gastric problems and colds. Mix it with hot water and honey and drink twice a day for five days to cure gastric problems. It contains 40% alcohol. Drink only one ounce an hour.

Alcohol helps to relax your mind if you drink only at the right time and consume only the right amount. Follow the above guidelines. If you drink too much alcohol you could have kidney, liver, hair, and brain stroke problems.

5 oz. Nutrition in Alcoholic Beverages				
Drink	Calorie	Protein	Carbohydrates	Iron
Red Table Wine	125	.1 g	3.84 g	4%
Chardonnay	121	.1 g	3.43 g	0
Sauvignon Blanc	122	.1 g	3.01 g	0
Riesling	122	.1 g	5.56 g	0
Muscat	124	.1 g	7.84 g	0
Beer	60	1.0 g	7.10 g	0
Johnny Walker Black Label Whiskey	330	0	0	0

HIGH-CALORIE FOODS

Do not consume too much high-calorie food. They will make you fat. Consuming too much fat and cholesterol will block your arteries. Eat responsibly.

One teaspoon of sugar contains 16 calories. One teaspoon of salt contains 2,325 milligrams of sodium. Too much salt causes high blood pressure. Check the level of calories in high-calorie foods before you eat them.

High Calorie Food per 100 grams					
Food	Calories	Fat	Protein	Carbohydrates	Cholesterol
Honey	304	0	0	82.4	0
Cheddar Cheese	403	33.14 g	24.9 g	1.89 g	105 mg
Cheesecake	321	22.5 g	5.5 g	25.5 g	55 mg
Ice Cream	201	10.72 g	3.52 g	24.9 g	40 mg
Sugar	387	0	0	99.98 g	0
Olive Oil	884	100 g	0	0	0
Butter	717	81.11 g	.85 g	.6 g	215 mg
Pork Fat	665	71 g	5.8 g	0	77 mg
Plain Donuts	198	10.67 g	2.35 g	23.36 g	17 mg

NEPALESE CULTURE

Nepal has many different tribes. Each has their separate beliefs and cuisines and culture. I will just speak of the Rai and Sherpa cultures here.

RAI CULTURE

Rai is a Kirat family, descended from the first king of Nepal. Today their occupations are Gurkhas and farmers. They worship the planet. They perform ceremonies for the Earth at the seed planting time in order to get a good harvest. The ceremony is called Sakela or Chandi. To perform Sakela all of the villages with their shamans and spiritual leaders get together at their desired locations. Shamans connect to the Divine and ask for a better harvest. The location must be on a water point, like a natural spring and must have a big tree and a special kind of snake, also called a nag, which is the Lord of the Earth. Only the shaman and his entourage can enter the serpent's domain. The area must be kept clean and respected. If the snake has laid many eggs, the harvest will be good. If the snake has laid fewer eggs, the harvest will not be as good.

During the ceremony everyone plays drums, sings songs and dances. All the children dance as well. They sing and play instruments along with their elders. They dance to request the Divine to give them a better environment for their crops. Their children learn automatically from their culture. They also prepare their own special food for the ceremony.

During the dance you sing and play instruments. You really forget yourself and connect with the higher dimensions. You forget about all of your problems. It gives you solidarity of the moment to enjoy. I wish everybody experienced this culture. It imparts happiness and refreshes your mind, body and soul.

After the harvest in Nepal we have four months in which to relax. We have parties. We have a good society. The father protects the house and family. The mother nurtures the family and society. The Himalayas are very clean, fresh and high, close to God. Living in a loving and respecting environment feels like heaven. I have shared my culture, spices and cuisine at the café with the local people of northern California. They would like to visit Nepal and I would like to take a group of people on a cultural and foody tour of Nepal.

The Rai worship the Planet through the Shaman (Bijuwa in Rai language). When Bijuwa dies, his spirit comes to a clean, honest, young boy or girl. That person becomes the new Bijuwa, who helps to connect the Divine for the community. Rais are honest and happy people. They do an earth ceremony during seed planting time.

Berkeley, California organizes the annual Himalayan Fair at Live Oak Park about the third week of May. This a celebration of seed planting. If you visit there you will see real cultural performances and different cuisines from Nepal, India, Tibet, Pakistan, and Bhutan. There are stalls for gifts from all of these areas.

I have not missed any of these fairs. It refreshes me meeting my friends and the food, drink, and dancing is so much fun.

SHERPA CULTURE

Sherpa celebrate the Losar, which is a new year about in the middle of March. They have special food, music and dance in the course of the party. They practice Buddhism, which cherishes peace, and they are very strong. They are the mountain heroes. Most of the Sherpas get reincarnated in the next life.

Tenzing Norgay Sherpa and Edmond Hillary climbed Mount Everest for the first time in 1953. The first lady to climb Everest was Junko Tabei, in 1975. She was from Japan. Everest is 27,029ft (8848 m.) high.

BUDDHA AND SHIVA MEDITATION CAVE AND MOUNTAIN
[Spiritual Destination]

Haleshi Mahadev is a cave five hours east from Kathmandu.

Shiva is a Divine person who has a power to change his looks if he wants, also called Mahadev. It was during Satya Yuga. He used to give a boon to his worshipers. Bhashmeshor worshiped with the intent to become the most powerful man in the world, but he abused his power and became violent and killed people. Mahadev ordered him to stop harming people, but drunk Bhashmeshor became a demon and chased Shiva. Mahadev escaped around the mountain but Bhashmeshor kept chasing him. Mahadev thrust his feet into the mountain making a hole which trapped the demon inside and Mahadev escaped. The demon was trapped in the hole and died. Today we can see the dead body of Bhashmeshor and the foot print on the wall that Shiva made. Mahadev dug another cave next to that hole for meditation. Still today Buddhist and Hindu people meditate in that cave and believe they get help. Because of this, it is the biggest holy place in Nepal. Buddha also meditated there. People believe Shiva and Buddha were the same person but have different roles. This incident occurred during the last stage of the Satya Yuga. Also this incident was recorded as divine and eternal. Inside that cave, there are original symbols of Shiva, Ganesha, Katike, Parbati. The Rinpoche Lama and the symbol of Kailash are also in that cave.

Temke is one of the most beautiful of the holy mountains close to the Haleshi, where Mahadev and many other divine energies used to meditate and hang out. There is a big stone and a tree. People do their rituals at that location. Today all the spiritual leaders and shamans have to visit there in order to complete their ceremonies. From this mountain we can see all of the Himalayas to the north and the Indian Ocean to the south. It is about four hours by bus, east from Haleshi. There are so many holy places in Nepal with many rivers, and the Nepalese respect all the religious practices. If you visit those two places you will observe the scene and understand a higher dimension of spirituality, and think twice before giving any boon to bad guy.

PHYSICAL LEADERSHIP [Trek to Everest Base Camp]

Walking one mile burns 70 calories. Running the same distance burns 150 calories. Exercising helps to alleviate cardiac conditions, type-2 diabetes, osteoporosis, obesity, depression and stabilizes the blood pressure. Working out is good for your soul.

Physical activity helps you to stay healthy and sleep soundly. Opportunities to see nature, like hills, mountains, rivers and the beautiful Himalayas will help you feel even better. Traveling to different countries is good for mindfulness. Princess Diana went to Nepal while she was separated from her marriage. She was refreshed from the people, culture and the mountains. Exercise makes the mind and body strong and the muscles tight. People will like you, especially your partner.

Nutrition is the key for sustaining high levels of exercise. Begin with walking. Walk fast, then progress to running slowly. Then run faster for one hour. This reduces belly fat to less than one inch. After running, do push-ups, pull-ups and sit-ups. These are upper-body exercises. Select a good running route and exercise area. Maintaining an exercise routine and traveling to different parts of the world will keep you fit. Nepal has the Himalayas, which have many hiking trails. The Annapurna Circuit and the Mt. Everest Circuit are the most popular hiking routes in the world. The Sherpas are the professional hiking guides in the Himalayas. It is necessary to hire a guide in the Himalayas. This program below will get you around the Mount Everest region. If you do this hiking, you will not regret it. When there is a will, there is a way.

Everest Sherpa Travel Package

Day 01 & 02: Preparation for travel. Acclimating to altitude.

Day 03: Kathmandu to Lukla (2886m.)

Fly from Kathmandu to Lukla (2886m.) which takes 30 minutes and trek from Lukla to Phakding (2640m.) which takes approximately three hours. You transfer to the domestic airport for your flight to Lukla. It is a small town with an airport. There are few tea shops, lodges, hotels and general stores. You begin today's trek from Lukla following a gentle climb up the mountainside on the left bank of the Dudh Koshi. Nupla (5885m) can be seen in the distance on the opposite bank, is a peak atop the Kongde Ridge. You descend a mountainside path that merges into your route to Everest, with views to a valley to your right; and at its far end, Kusum Kang (6367m.) The Dudh Kosi approaches as you pass a Mani wall and arrive at Ghat teahouse. You continue along a small path with many climbs and descents following the left bank of Dudh Koshi to Phakding.

Day 04: Phakding to Monjo (2835m.)

Trek from Phakding to Monjo (2835m.) and it takes approximately two hours. From Phakding you cross the river and head up valley following porters from the south, ferrying supplies to Namche. The trail keeps close to the river valley and is lined with a beautiful blue pine and rhododendron forest that is very spectacular in the spring months when the flowers are in bloom. You cross the Dudh Koshi at Benkar where there are tantalizing glimpses of the snow peaks Kusum Kanguru (6369m) and Thamserku (6623m). From here it is only a short walk to Monjo (2835m) where you arrive in time for lunch. You spend the night in Monjo with the afternoon free, with the opportunity to do some exploring around the village. The day has been deliberately kept short to aid acclimatization, which is a very important process.

Day 05: Monjo to Namche Bazaar (3440m.)

Trek from Monjo to Namche Bazaar (3440m.) which takes about three hours. Today the walking is a little tougher and includes the steep ascent to Namche Bazaar. From Monjo, it is a short walk to the entrance of the National Park before you cross the Dudh Kosi, to reach Jorsale (2805m.). The trek continues upstream on generally flat terrain, crossing back to the right bank, to the confluence of the Bhote Koshi and Dudh Koshi rivers; it is here that you start the steep ascent to Namche Bazaar. After crossing a large and stable suspension bridge high above the river you slowly ascend at a steady pace towards Namche. There are some fantastic photographic opportunities as the peaks of Everest, Lhotse, Nuptse, Ama Dablam and Tawache (6542m.) come into view for the first time. After arriving in Namche, you enjoy lunch, with the afternoon is free to bargain in the shops for Tibetan artifacts, or relax and marvel at the beautiful scenery.

Day 06: Rest day at Namche Bazaar for acclimatization

Rest day at Namche Bazaar for acclimatization and excursion around the places.
Namche is tucked away between two ridges amidst the giant peaks of the Khumbu and has an abundance of lodges, tea shops and souvenir shops as well as a magnificent outlook. It is an ideal place to spend a rest day for acclimatization to the high altitude before heading off towards Tyangboche. For the acclimatization you walk up to Khumjung where you can visit a monastery. Khumjung is densely populated by a Sherpa community. You can also enjoy the splendid views of Everest, Ama Dablam, Thamserku, Nuptse, Lhotse, Tawche, Kwangde and so on. Or you can have an hour walk up to the Syangboche (3800m.) where Everest View Hotel is situated above Namche for the outstanding view of Everest, Nuptse, Lhotse, Ama Dablam, Thamserku and Kusum Kangaru. There are also good views from the National Park Centre and Museum just above the town. This museum exhibits Sherpa culture.

Day 07: Namche Bazaar to Tyangboche (3867m.)

Trek from Namche Bazaar to Tyangboche (3867m.) which takes approximately five and half hours. From

Namche, you climb towards the park headquarters and follow a contouring trail high above the Dudh Koshi River. Above Namche the route to Thyangboche becomes visible with the monastery seen below the summit of Everest and surrounded by Himalayan peaks. On today's walk there are opportunities to spot the local wildlife, including the beautiful Danphe Pheasant often seen among the birch and silver fir forest between Shanasa and Trashinga, and Himalayan Thar on the high ground above the trail. After reaching the re-forestation nursery at Trashinga, the trail drops steeply to cross the Dudh Koshi at Phunkitenga (3250m.), where you take lunch. In the afternoon you pass water-driven prayer wheels and ascend, initially steeply, through pine, fir, black juniper and rhododendron forest towards Thyangboche. The monastery and lodge are located in a beautiful meadow surrounded by towering Himalayan peaks in a truly peaceful and tranquil setting. The most notable peaks seen from here are Kantega, Ama Dablam (perhaps the most beautiful peak in the region) and, of course, Mount Everest.

Day 08: Tyangboche to Shanasa (3670m.)

Trek from Tyangboche to Shanasa (3670m.) which takes almost two and one-half hours. In the 17th century AD, the Lama Sange Dorjee, from Tibet's Rongbuk Monastery, according to legend, founded the monastery here. It was destroyed by an earthquake in 1933, rebuilt and again badly damaged by fire in 1989. Construction of the present monastery was completed in 1992. You have a full morning at Thyangboche to visit the monastery and the nearby museum. There is a small entrance fee for the museum and a small donation to the monastery is appreciated. In the afternoon you retrace your steps down hill through the beautiful forest of juniper, rhododendron and fir to Phunkitenga. After you cross the Dudh Koshi, you ascend steeply to Trashinga. From here the trail contours high above the valley to Shanasa where you spend the night. Here Tibetan traders, resident in the area, have numerous "artifacts" and worthwhile traditional souvenirs for sale.

Day 09: Shanasa to Monjo (2835m.)

Trek from Shanasa to Monjo (2835m.) which takes approximately five and one-half hours. The villages of Kunde and Khumjung are only a short trek off the main trail and are well worth a visit. Khumjung has a beautiful monastery and Kunde has a small hospital run by Sir Edmund Hillary's Himalayan Trust and you shall return to Namche via this route. The walk also heads past the Everest View Hotel and the Shyangboche airstrip before dropping into Namche where you take lunch. In the afternoon you descend steeply and then walk along the river bank back to Jorsale where you leave the national park before continuing on to your lodge at Monjo where you stay overnight.

Day 10: Monjo to Lukla (2886m.)

Trek from Monjo to Lukla (2886m.) which takes about four hours. You re-trace your steps along the Dudh Koshi, crossing the western bank at Benkar. It is a beautiful and easy walk through blue pine and rhododendron forest, back-dropped with views of Kusum Kangaru. An early lunch will be taken at Phakding and in the afternoon you ascend out of the river valley back to the airstrip and you are offered lodge accommodation at

Lukla. In the evening, a farewell dinner may be followed by a few celebratory drinks and dancing with Sherpa companions.

Day 11: Morning flight to Kathmandu from Lukla

Enjoying your last glimpse of the mountains you have recently visited for one last time on the 35-minute scenic flight back to Kathmandu. Overnight at a hotel.

Day 12: Leisure day in Kathmandu.

It's also a spare day in case of bad weather in Lukla, or

A free day in Kathmandu where you can shop. In the evening we will drive you to a farewell dinner with cultural dance.

Day 13: Transfer for your final flight departure.

The trip ends, an Everest Sherpa Travel Airport Representative will drop you to the Kathmandu international airport for your flight departure from Nepal.

Trip Cost Includes:

- All domestic flights and hotel/airport transfer

- All accommodation and meals during the trek

- All costs for Sherpa leader, Sharps, assistant trek leaders and porters; including their salary, insurance, equipment, flight, food and lodging

- A 4 star hotel in Kathmandu with breakfast

- Sightseeing in Kathmandu and all entry fees

- All ground transport in private vehicles

- A four-season sleeping bag

- Welcome and farewell dinner

- All necessary paper work and permits

- A comprehensive medical kit

- All government and local taxes

Trip Cost Does Not Include:

- Nepal visa fees

- International Airfare

- Excess baggage charges

- Lunch and evening meals in Kathmandu

- Travel and rescue insurance

- Personal expenses (phone calls, laundry, bar bills or extra porters)

- Tips for guides and porters

NOTE: The above information is a guide and standard template of what we provide. The trek can be customized at your request to accommodate your specific requirements.

Tengboche

Everest Base Camp

Hillary Step

This is the hardest part of the climb on the way to Everest

POWERFUL TIPS FOR PERFECT HEALTH IN MIND AND BODY

1. Check your RDA every day. Examine your skin and body fat when you shower. Feel your spirit. You should be happy, light and fresh, peaceful and charming. Measure your happiness every day. Good food and exercise is the key to this goal.

2. To the new generation: This world is changing for the better and for the worst, for both food and mind. There are healthy and non-healthy foods. Some of the new generation has problems with bad food habits. Parents, doctors and teachers should control those problems by combining solutions. The new generation also needs to learn equality, compassion, forgiveness, peace, sexuality, pleasure, happiness and meditation. Young people must also understand the distractive powers of greed, ego, selfishness, emotional decisions, pride and entrapment. If you learn a new thing every day and learn from all of your mistakes, you can upgrade your life. You can be wise sooner.

3. For sleepless nights (insomnia) know that eating high-calorie foods can cause sleep loss. You must burn calories by exercise or dieting. Then you will sleep more easily.

4. Habit of the habit, pain of the pain. Eating and drinking too much will cause you to lose your health. Eating too much can cause diabetes, cancer, heart attacks and many other sicknesses. Drinking too much damages your liver, kidneys and eyes, including brain strokes. Eat and drink for pleasure and not for distraction, but for your health.

5. Food for taste: Food prepared by a farmer with a passion for raising plants and animals produces food that is high in quality. You must always shop at reputable local organic food markets that sell high-quality produce. Cooking with fresh spices and seasonings will increase the flavor of the food. Signature dishes will always make more friends.

6. We all can maintain our space by making universal rules, laws and regulations and showing our respect for family, society, the world, and the universe to establish boundaries. These days space is in trouble because people don't understand the boundaries. We have to work on it. We can take a minute to think and improve ourselves and the world.

7. Explore cuisine and culture. Nepal is a multi-tribal and multicultural country. Every tribe has a different cuisine and culture. Nepalese popular cuisine is called "chourasi banjan bhojan." That means 84 different dishes. Sherpas living in the high Himalayas eat hot and spicy foods, like yak, vegetables (mostly potatoes) and grains. People who live in the middle Himalayas eat medium to hot spices. They are Rai, Limbu, Magar, Tamang, Gurung and Newar. They eat buffalo, pig and lamb. They do not eat beef. People who live in

the south part of Nepal are called Madhesh. They consume less spice. They eat chicken and duck. Brahman and Chhetri are usually vegetarians, but some like goat meat and dairy foods.

Conclusion: There is great variety in the cuisine and culture in Nepal. The people of Nepal respect foreigners. It is good to visit Nepal and Asia and experience the cuisine and cultures of the people who live there. We all can learn and upgrade ourselves and the community. Thank you for reading my book. If you find this useful, please share with your friends and family. You can contact me on my email: makarrai954822@gmail.com

Made in the USA
Columbia, SC
21 November 2018